The Story of Islam

Rob Lloyd Jones

Designed by Karen Tomlins

History consultant: Dr. M. F. Elshayyal,
the Markfield Institute of Higher Education

Reading consultant: Alison Kelly, Roehampton University

Edited by Jane Chisholm

First published in 2007 by Usborne Publishing Ltd,
Usborne House, 83-85 Saffron Hill, London EC1N 8RT, England.
www.usborne.com

ACKNOWLEDGEMENTS

Cover © **CORBIS** (Steve Allen/Brand X); © **AKG Images** p24, pp30-31 (Jean-Louis
Nou), p36, p46, p58 (Cameraphoto); © **Alamy** pp42-43 (Visual Arts Library, London); ©
The Art Archive p15 (Topkapi Museum Istanbul /Harper Collins Publishers) pp44-45
(Victoria and Albert Museum London /Sally Chappell); © **Bridgeman Art Library** pp2-3
(Victoria and Albert Museum, London), pp6-7 (Guildhall Art Gallery, City of London), p14
(The Trustees of the Chester Beatty Library, Dublin), pp26-27 (Louvre, Paris), pp32-33
(British Library Board, All Rights Reserved), pp34-35 (Bristol City Museum and Art Library,
UK), p38 (University Library, Istanbul), p42 (Victoria and Albert Museum, London), p47
(Bibliotheque Nationale, Paris), p53 (Topkapi Palace Museum, Istanbul), pp54-55 (Stapleton
Collection, UK), p57, pp58-59 (Topkapi Palace Museum), pp60-61 (Museu Maritim
Atarazanas, Barcelona); © **British Museum** p28l; © **CORBIS** p1 (Mast Irham/epa), p9
(Amit Bhargava), pp12-13 (Zainal Abd Halim/Reuters), pp16-19 (Kazuyoshi Nomachi), p20-
21 (Smithsonian Institute), p37 (Jose Fuste Raga), p39 (Austrian Archives), pp48-49 (Bob
Krist), pp50-51 (Archivo Iconografico, S.A.), pp62-63 (Jon Hicks); © **Dover Publications**
pp40-14, p64; © **Photolibrary Group** p29b; © **Michael Holford** pp22-23; © **Peter Sanders**
pp10-11, p29; © **Werner Foreman Archive** p50-51t

This scene, painted in
the 18th century, shows
Muslims praying together
in a mosque in India.

Contents

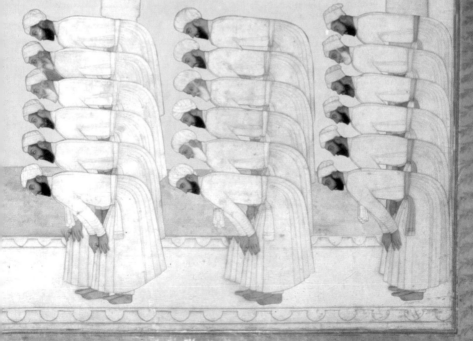

The first part of this book tells the story of a man named Muhammad, the most important prophet, or messenger, in the religion of Islam. Followers of Islam usually add the words 'peace be upon him' each time they say his name. This phrase is written in Arabic on page 5.

MEDITERRANEAN
SEA

•Damascus

SYRIA

•Baghdad

IRAQ

•Jerusalem

•Cairo

EGYPT

• Medina

• Badr

• Mecca

ARABIA

RED
SEA

AFRICA

ARABIAN
SEA

Most of the events in the
early history of Islam took
place in the towns and cities
shown in the map above.

Chapter 1

The land of Arabia

In the 6th century, most of Arabia was a vast and empty desert. For miles, the ground was either dry and cracked, or filled with rolling sand dunes and jagged rocky peaks. The only water was found at natural springs, called oases, which dotted the desert. Small towns grew up around them, and shepherds came to graze their herds of goats and sheep.

Many Arabians were nomads, spending their lives moving their animals from one oasis to the next. Others crossed the desert with long lines of camels, known as caravans, carrying sweet-smelling spices, luxury cloth or exotic perfumes, which they sold from town to town.

One of the largest trading places was Mecca, an oasis town near the west coast of Arabia. Hundreds of traders came here each day to do business. But other people came on holy journeys, or pilgrimages, to a large stone temple named

the Kaaba. Most Arabians worshipped lots of different gods, which they believed lived in the rocks and trees, and the Kaaba contained hundreds of altars and shrines dedicated to them.

Although all Arabians spoke the same language, they belonged to different tribes, who were often at war with each other. They ransacked each other's caravans in the desert, and even murdered members of rival tribes. But in the 7th century, all this changed thanks to just one man.

His name was Muhammad.

Scenes like this, of a camel caravan resting in the desert, were common in Arabia during the 7th century.

Chapter 2

The life of Muhammad

U ntil he was about forty years old, Muhammad
lived a similar life to many other people in
Mecca. As a boy, he worked on trade caravans
belonging to his uncle, Abu Talib, then for a rich
widow named Khadijah, who he later married. The
work was hard, criss-crossing the baking desert,
often with little food or water. But Muhammad
loved sitting by the campfires at night, listening
to traders' stories about love, history and war.

Muhammad was popular and trusted by
everyone. He could have lived the comfortable life
of a wealthy trader, but he was troubled by the
world around him. In particular, he hated the way

8

many rich people spent their days gambling, drinking and fighting. They treated women and children terribly, cheated the poor, and often lay drunk in doorways.

Muhammad began to spend his spare time in a cave on a mountain outside the town, thinking and praying about the problems in the world. Sometimes he sat there for an entire month, while his daughters brought him food and water every few days.

The customs of many Arab traders haven't changed much since the time of Muhammad. Here, a group of camel traders swap stories by campfire at night.

One day, in around the year 610, Muhammad was sitting alone in his cave when he heard the voice of an angel speaking to him. The angel told Muhammad that he was one of God's messengers, or prophets. He should tell everyone that there was only one God, named Allah in Arabic, and that this God would judge everyone when they died and send them to heaven or hell.

Over the next few years, Muhammad received more and more messages from God. Sometimes he saw visions of an angel. Other times, he heard

This cave, on a mountain close to Mecca, is where Muslims believe Muhammad had his first revelation from God.

voices in his head. They told him that people should be kind to their parents, generous to strangers and pray to God to forgive the things they had done wrong. Muhammad memorized the messages, and repeated them to his friends, to his family, and to anyone in Mecca who would listen. The people who believed Muhammad called the messages 'revelations'. They wrote them on pieces of dried animal skin, and carried them everywhere they went.

The revelations said that believers in the messages should be called Muslims, which means those who submit to the will of God. Their new religion became known as Islam – submission to God's will.

"There is no God but Allah," the Muslims declared, "and Muhammad is the messenger of God."

Others weren't so convinced. Many Meccan businessmen realized that if people rejected the gods worshipped at the Kaaba shrine, pilgrims would stop coming to the city.

"They won't rent our hotel rooms," they complained, "or drink in our inns. How will we make any money?"

So they accused Muhammad of lying, and persecuted his followers. Some Muslims were arrested, others were beaten, and one was even left to die in the desert, crushed beneath a huge rock.

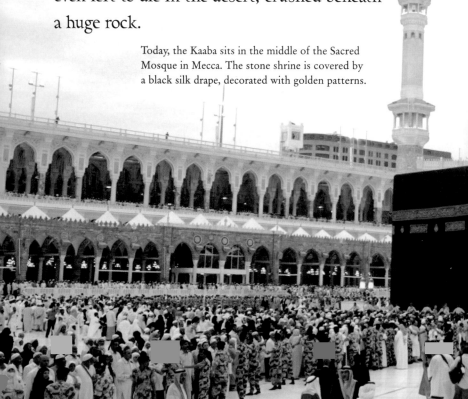

Today, the Kaaba sits in the middle of the Sacred Mosque in Mecca. The stone shrine is covered by a black silk drape, decorated with golden patterns.

A few years later, in 619, both Muhammad's wife Khadijah and his uncle Abu Talib became ill and died. Things seemed bleak for Muhammad. But the next year he described to his followers how an angel had carried him on a miraculous flight to heaven, where he spoke to other prophets such as Abraham, Moses, and Jesus. This incredible journey gave Muhammad strength to carry on.

Until now, Muhammad had been protected by his uncle, who belonged to a powerful tribe called the Quraysh. But, now that his uncle was dead, even the Quraysh turned against Muhammad, sending assassins to kill him as he slept. Luckily, Muhammad learned of the plot, and escaped.

This 18th century painting shows the first mosque to be built in Medina.

By now, Mecca had become too dangerous for Muhammad. In 622, he and his followers moved to Yathrib, an oasis town 320km (180 miles) to the north. Muhammad already had some supporters there, and they welcomed him into their homes.

Muhammad stayed in Yathrib for the next two years. He built a place of worship for Muslims, known as a mosque, and lived beside it a simple house made of mud bricks. He continued to receive revelations from God about how people should live, and more and more people began to listen. Soon, Muhammad had become the leader of the entire town, which later changed its name to 'Madinat-al-nabi' (City of the Prophet), or Medina for short.

The Meccans, though, were still determined to destroy Islam. When Muhammad left Mecca for Medina, they offered a hundred camels to anyone who could bring him back, dead or alive. Now, they attacked the families of other Muslims who had moved from the city, stealing their houses and selling their property.

Muhammad decided to fight back. In March 624, he led over 300 followers to capture a Meccan caravan carrying Muslim belongings. Furious, the Meccans sent an army against them, and the two sides fought near a well in the desert named Badr. Muhammad's followers were outnumbered almost three to one, but they still drove the Meccans back to their city. The Muslims had become a powerful fighting force.

Many Muslim soldiers rode on camels to the battle at Badr, as shown in this 14th century painting.

Soon, it was too powerful for the Meccans. In 630, Muhammad gathered an army of over 10,000 Muslims and marched to their city. The Meccans surrendered with little fighting. Cheered by his followers, Muhammad marched through the streets to the Kaaba temple, where he destroyed the altars to all the old gods. From now on, the Kaaba was dedicated only to Allah.

The conquest of Mecca was a spectacular success for Islam, but the effort left Muhammad exhausted. He returned to Medina, but fell ill with fever in 632, and died in his home in June that year. His followers turned his house into a tomb, and the mosque beside it became one of the most sacred sites in their new religion.

Muhammad's tomb lies within this huge mosque, known as the Mosque of the Prophet, in the holy city of Medina.

Chapter 3

The Five Pillars of Islam

The history of Islam after Muhammad's death is an incredible story of empires rising and falling as the religion spread around the globe.

Today, it is one of the largest religions in the world. Some Muslims argue about different aspects of their faith, but they all lead their lives according to the same basic customs and beliefs. These are known as the Five Pillars of Islam.

The first pillar is simply a declaration, called the *shahadah*, in which a person states his belief that there is no true God except Allah, and that Muhammad is the messenger of Allah. The second pillar of Islam is special prayers, or *salah*, which Muslims are expected to make five times every day, facing in the direction of Mecca. They also pray together each Friday in mosques.

The third pillar is charity. Each year, Muslims are supposed to give a percentage of whatever money they have saved to help the poor. They believe that this money, known as *zakah*, will help make their own wealth pure.

Muslims commemorate the month in which Muhammad received his first revelation from God by avoiding all food and drink between sunrise and sunset every single day. This fasting, which they call *sawm*, helps them feel closer to God, and reminds them how lucky they are to have food. The month is called Ramadan, and it ends in a festival of feasting and prayer called Eid al-Fitr, or Breaking of the Fast.

Thousands of Muslim women arrive at
the Mosque of the Prophet in Medina
during the annual Hajj, or pilgrimage.

Finally, all Muslims who can are required to
make a holy journey, or pilgrimage, to Mecca
once in their lives. This pilgrimage is called the
Hajj, and is the fifth pillar of Islam.

As well as these five pillars, some Muslims also celebrate significant events in Muhammad's life. These include his birthday, his miraculous journey to heaven, which they call the *mi-raj,* and his journey from Mecca to Medina.

But most important of all are the revelations given to Muhammad by God. During Muhammad's lifetime, his followers wrote down the exact words of these messages. Together, they form a book known as the Qur'an, which means 'to be read'.

The Qur'an contains 114 chapters, or *suras,* written in Arabic. As well as praising God, the *suras* give Muslims guidance on aspects of their everyday life, such as marriage, law, or charity. Qur'ans are always placed on stands to avoid them being damaged. Making a beautiful handwritten copy of the book is regarded as an act of great worship.

To make sure the revelations are the same as when Muhammad first heard them, not one word of the Qur'an has been changed since it was first written down.

وَأَمَّا مَنْ خَافَ مَقَامَ رَبِّهِ وَنَهَى النَّفْسَ عَنِ الْهَوَى فَإِنَّ الْجَنَّةَ هِيَ الْمَأْوَى

يَسْأَلُونَكَ عَنِ السَّاعَةِ أَيَّانَ مُرْسَاهَا فِيمَ أَنْتَ مِنْ ذِكْرَاهَا إِلَى رَبِّكَ مُنْتَهَاهَا إِنَّمَا

أَنْتَ مُنْذِرُ مَنْ يَخْشَاهَا كَأَنَّهُمْ يَوْمَ يَرَوْنَهَا لَمْ يَلْبَثُوا إِلَّا عَشِيَّةً أَوْ ضُحَاهَا

سُورَةُ عَبَسَ اثْنَانِ وَأَرْبَعُونَ آيَةً مَكِّيَّةٌ

بِسْمِ اللَّهِ الرَّحْمَٰنِ الرَّحِيمِ

عَبَسَ وَتَوَلَّى أَنْ جَاءَهُ الْأَعْمَى وَمَا يُدْرِيكَ لَعَلَّهُ يَزَّكَّى أَوْ يَذَّكَّرُ فَتَنْفَعَهُ

الذِّكْرَى أَمَّا مَنِ اسْتَغْنَى فَأَنْتَ لَهُ تَصَدَّى وَمَا عَلَيْكَ أَلَّا يَزَّكَّى وَأَمَّا مَنْ

جَاءَكَ يَسْعَى وَهُوَ يَخْشَى فَأَنْتَ عَنْهُ تَلَهَّى كَلَّا إِنَّهَا تَذْكِرَةٌ فَمَنْ شَاءَ ذَكَرَهُ

فِي صُحُفٍ مُكَرَّمَةٍ مَرْفُوعَةٍ مُطَهَّرَةٍ بِأَيْدِي سَفَرَةٍ كِرَامٍ بَرَرَةٍ قُتِلَ

الْإِنْسَانُ مَا أَكْفَرَهُ مِنْ أَيِّ شَيْءٍ خَلَقَهُ مِنْ نُطْفَةٍ خَلَقَهُ فَقَدَّرَهُ

Early handwritten copies of the Qur'an were often
decorated like this, with beautiful patterns and colours.

21

Chapter 4

The first caliphs

Muhammad's followers were stunned when he died. How could he leave them, they asked. After all, he was their prophet. One man even drew his sword, refusing to allow anyone to bury Muhammad's body. Other Muslims turned to Muhammad's closest friend, a man named Abu Bakr, for answers. He had known Muhammad since they were young, and had been one of the first to hear the prophet's revelations.

"Muhammad is indeed dead," he told a crowd in Medina, "but God is alive and will never die!"

"But who will lead us now?" people asked.

There was no easy answer – Muhammad hadn't left clear advice about who should follow him as leader of the Muslim community. Eventually Abu Bakr was chosen, and given the title *caliph*, which means successor.

"I have been chosen by you as your leader," he said, "though I am no better than any of you. If I do well, give me support. If I do wrong, set me right."

This painting shows Muslims gathered in Medina to listen to Ali, the fourth caliph of Islam.

Muslim pilgrims came from all over the new Islamic empire
to the holy cities of Mecca and Medina. Here, their camels
are loaded with gifts for the caliphs.

Three more caliphs followed Abu Bakr over
the next thirty years – Umar, Uthman and
Muhammad's cousin, Ali. These four leaders were
known as the Rightly Guided Caliphs, because

they led according to Muhammad's example, wearing simple clothes and living in simple houses, without guards. They used the words of the Qur'an to guide them in the way they led the Muslim community.

By the time Abu Bakr died in 634, almost all of Arabia had converted to Islam. But the Rightly Guided Caliphs saw it as their holy duty to carry the message of the Qur'an even further. To do so, they built an army.

Marching from Arabia, a 4,000-strong Islamic force defeated the army of the Christian Byzantine empire to conquer Syria and Palestine. Then they marched against the Persians in Mesopotamia, defeating them too. The Muslim soldiers were often outnumbered, but they were fired with religious passion. The Qur'an promised that any Muslim who died for his religion would go to heaven. Charging into battle, they showered enemy ranks with arrows and spears.

"Allah is great!" they cried. "There is no God but Allah!"

The spread of Islam from Arabia during the
rule of the Rightly Guided Caliphs

The caliphs never forced people in conquered
lands to become Muslims. Some people converted
to Islam because it seemed simpler than religions
that worshipped many gods. Others had grown
tired of heavy taxes under previous rulers, and
hoped for better treatment from the Muslims.

Those people who didn't convert to Islam had to pay an extra tax, which meant they would be protected by the Muslim army. So, eventually, most people did adopt the new religion.

Islam was also spread by Muslim traders. Leading huge camel caravans, these men braved the scorching desert sun and treacherous mountain passes to carry their goods beyond the edges of the new Islamic empire. They took perfume, pottery and grain, and returned to Arabia with gold, glass and ivory from places as far away as west Africa and India. To make their journeys easier, they built hundreds of shelters, called caravansaries, where they could rest and feed their camels.

Weary camel caravans often stopped for the night in shelters like this in the desert.

But the great new Islamic empire did not stay united for long. After the death of the third caliph, Uthman, in 656, Muslims began to argue about who should be the next leader. Many believed that it should be the person who was most likely to follow the example and traditions of Muhammad, known as the *sunna*. These became known as Sunni Muslims.

Others felt the caliph could only be chosen from descendants of Muhammad himself. They believed the prophet's cousin, Ali, should lead them. Later, this group became known as Shi'at Ali – the followers of Ali – or Shi'ites, for short. The Shi'ites refused to accept that Abu Bakr, Umar and Uthman had been real caliphs, and always regarded Ali as the first.

An army of Shi'ite Muslims carried this golden emblem into battle against Sunni troops in 680.

After Ali's death in 661, a tribe of Sunni Muslims known as the Umayyads took control of the Islamic empire. They expanded Muslim lands as far as India in the east and Spain in the west – almost a quarter of the way around the world.

A golden coin minted during the period of Umayyad rule

Arabic became the official language of the empire, new Islamic coins were created, and there was even a postal system.

The Umayyads built dozens of spectacular mosques during their reign, including this, the Dome of the Rock, in Jerusalem.

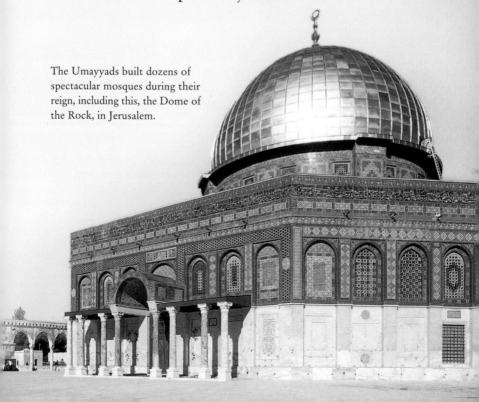

But, instead of behaving like caliphs, the Umayyads acted like kings. They moved their capital away from Mecca to Damascus, in Syria, and lived in lavish palaces. People believed they spent their days drinking wine surrounded by beautiful women, which was against Islamic law.

To fund their extravagant lifestyles, the Umayyads taxed non-Muslims more than ever before. Previous caliphs had given this tax money to the poor, so the Umayyads became very unpopular. They had betrayed the spirit of Islam.

The Umayyads no longer had such a powerful army to protect themselves, either. The soldiers who had helped build the empire had settled down as farmers, and refused to fight any more.

In 750, a group of Shi'ite Muslims named the Abbasids – who were decended from Muhammad's uncle, Abbas – raised an army of supporters and defeated the Umayyads at the Battle of the Great Zab. The Abbasids declared themselves the new caliphs. This was the beginning of a period of great wealth and culture that became known as the Golden Age of Islam.

The Umayyads built this huge mosque in Damascus, decorated with lavish golden mosaics.

Chapter 5

The Golden Age of Islam

Like the Umayyads, the Abbasids decided to create a new capital for their new empire. From 762, they turned a small fishing village nestled on the banks of the river Tigris, in modern Iraq, into the most spectacular city in the world. It was called Baghdad.

Rising from the desert like a mirage, Baghdad was an incredible sight. It was built in a giant circle, two miles across and enclosed by huge walls lined with guard towers. Over a million Muslims moved to the city. They lived among hundreds of mosques, thousands of public baths, lush landscaped gardens and great bustling market places, known as bazaars.

Baghdad would actually have been even larger than this 17th century engraving shows, with many more palaces and mosques.

Stalls in the bazaars were packed with exotic goods from around the world – silk from China, rubies and silver from India, leather from Spain and animal furs from Russia. Many Muslims now abandoned their desert traditions, choosing to sleep on mattresses rather than the floor, to eat at tables, and drink from porcelain cups. They also enjoyed new games and sports, such as chess and backgammon, which had been learned from Persia.

Baghdad also developed into the world's leading city for learning. Muhammad had urged Muslims to learn more about God's universe, and now Muslim scholars and scientists set out to do so. A huge library was built, named the House of Wisdom, where books from Ancient Greece, in particular, were translated into Arabic, and ideas were gathered from all over the empire.

Sprawling covered markets, or bazaars, like this can still be found in many Muslim cities.

Medical texts like this one gave Muslim
doctors advice about how to prepare medicines.

The most popular subject was medicine.
Muhammad said that "for every disease, Allah
has given a cure," so now Muslim scientists
tried to find them.

The best-known Muslim doctor of the Golden
Age was Al-Razi, or Rhazes as he is known in
the West. Rhazes wrote hundreds of medical
texts detailing symptoms and cures for diseases
such as smallpox and measles. His books were
used to teach other Muslim doctors, who
performed surgery on ears, eyes and throats,
hundreds of years before operations like these
were attempted anywhere else in the world.

Muslim mathematicians introduced a new system of counting from India to replace the old Roman numerals. This made subtraction and multiplication easier, helping people to keep more accurate accounts, and farmers to measure their fields more precisely.

Muslim scholars also increased their understanding of lines and angles, known as geometry. Architects used this knowledge to design grand palaces with pillars and domes, and mosques surrounded by spiralling towers called minarets. Engineers built huge wheels to draw water from rivers, long aqueducts to carry it to towns, and complex drainage systems to take it away.

Minarets can be found in many different styles on mosques around the world. These decorate a mosque in Cairo, Egypt.

Early Muslim astronomers are shown here using astrolabes, a large globe, and other scientific instruments in an observatory in Istanbul, Turkey.

Astronomical observatories were built in Baghdad, where scholars studied the night sky. For centuries, nomads and traders in the desert had used the stars to guide them, but now new scientific instruments were invented which made navigation much easier and more accurate. These included the magnetic compass and the astrolabe, which measured the angle between a star and the Earth. Devices like these also helped guide pilgrims on their holy journeys to Mecca, and were later used by European explorers who discovered America.

Bronze astrolabes like this were used by astronomers to measure the height of a star or planet in the sky.

Other skills learned from around the empire included printing using blocks of wood, steel-making, and new ways of dying materials. In 751, Muslims also discovered how to make paper, which they were taught by captured Chinese soldiers. A new style of Islamic art began to emerge too. Muslims discouraged art that showed God, or living creatures – particularly human beings. They felt that no one could possibly imagine what God was like, or capture the magnificence of his creations.

Another reason for not showing pictures of humans was that Muslims didn't want people to start worshipping these images rather than God. Instead, Baghdad's grandest palaces and mosques were decorated with elaborate flowing lines and interweaving patterns, known as arabesques, often painted in deep blue or turquoise. Palaces were filled with exquisite mosaics or ornately carved stone and marble. They were furnished with beautifully patterned carpets woven from silk and bright golden thread.

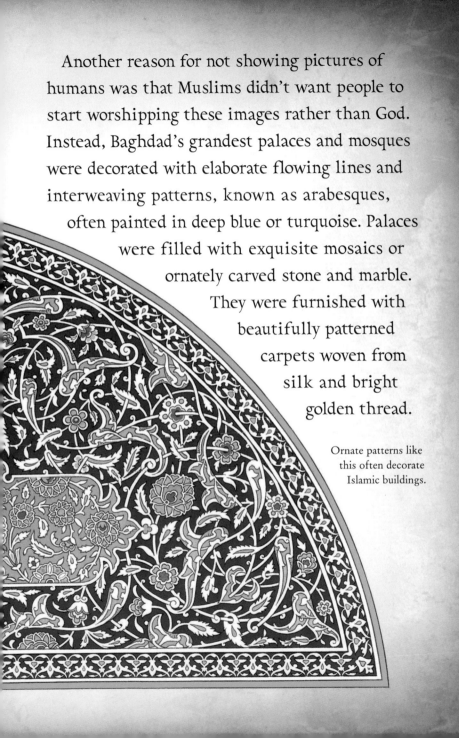

Ornate patterns like this often decorate Islamic buildings.

This might look like a vase, but it's actually a glass lamp, decorated with words from the Qur'an, written in calligraphy.

The most common feature of Islamic art, though, is decorative handwriting, known as calligraphy. Written using the tips of reeds dipped in ink, calligraphy was regarded as one of the most skilled art forms. Muslims used it to write copies of the Qur'an because they believed it helped express the beauty of God's revelations. But calligraphy was also used to decorate buildings, paintings and even everyday objects such as vases and plates.

The Golden Age was also a great period for Islamic literature. The best-known example is *Thousand and One Nights*, a collection of historical tales, love stories and poems from all over the empire.

Some of these stories feature the Abbasid caliphs themselves, as well as fictional characters who have since become famous, such as Aladdin, Sinbad the Sailor and the beautiful princess Scheherazade. They describe Baghdad as a fairy-tale city of real and imaginary delights – princes on white horses, flying carpets, genies in lamps, dancing girls and magicians.

Scenes like this, of a prince riding a flying carpet, were inspired by the stories in *Thousand and One Nights*.

But while the Abbasids lived like kings at the heart of their glorious new city, the rest of their empire began to crumble. In 868, a dynasty of Shi'ite Muslims descended from Muhammad's daughter Fatima seized power in Egypt. The Fatimids declared themselves the new caliphs, and built Cairo into a capital city to rival even Baghdad in size and magnificence.

In the east, too, new powers were rising. A fierce Muslim tribe from central Asia named the Seljuk Turks swept through Syria, capturing Baghdad in 1055. Their leader, a commander named Togrul Beg, declared himself sultan, or ruler. For the next 200 years, the Abbasids were forced to do whatever the Seljuks commanded.

After defeating the Abbasids, the Seljuk army continued west and captured the ancient city of Jerusalem in 1071. This sparked outrage among Christians in Europe. To them, Jerusalem was a holy city, where Jesus had lived and died. Over the next 200 years, tens of thousands of Christian knights marched in a series of holy wars, known as the crusades, to recapture Jerusalem from the Muslims.

In the end, though, the crusades achieved little other than to create a division between Christians and Muslims that lasts even until today.

The city of Jerusalem, below, contains sites that are sacred to both Muslims and Christians.

Throughout this turmoil, Baghdad remained a glorious city of culture and learning. But, in the middle of the 13th century, a tribe of nomadic warriors rose to power in central Asia, determined to conquer new land. Their name was the Mongols, which means 'the invincible ones'.

Led by a savage warlord named Genghis Khan, the Mongols attacked city after city, with hordes of Chinese archers, great wooden towers called siege engines, and barrels of gunpowder. They struck fear wherever they rode, torturing prisoners and burning cities to the ground. Baghdad was no exception.

The great Mongol leader Genghis Khan is shown here seated on his throne.

Mongol troops charge into battle in this scene painted almost a hundred years after Genghis Khan's death.

Genghis Khan's grandson, Hulagu, invaded the city in 1258, looting the palaces, and ransacking the House of Wisdom. Books that had been gathered over hundreds of years were set alight, or tossed into the rivers. Over a million Muslims were dragged from their homes and slaughtered in the streets. The last Abbasid caliph, Al-Musta'sim, was tied to the back of a horse and dragged through the city, before being kicked to death. It was the end of the greatest era in the history of Islam.

Chapter 6
The spread of Islam

After the fall of Baghdad, Islam continued to spread around the world. Even the Mongols became Muslims eventually. In the 14th century, the Mongol leader Tamerlane built a great new capital at Samarkand, in Turkestan. He conquered lands from Arabia to India, massacring thousands along the way. In Delhi, he had the skulls of 80,000 victims piled up against the city gates. Despite his ferocity, religion was very important to Tamerlane, and he built hundreds of mosques throughout his lands. He died in 1405, and his empire collapsed soon after.

In the 16th century, one of Tamerlane's decendants, a Mongol prince named Babur, founded a Muslim dynasty named the Mughals, which ruled over parts of India for over 200 years. The Mughals produced many great works of art and architecture, the most famous of which is the Taj Mahal, a spectacular tomb for the wife of the Mughal emperor Shah Jahan.

Today, the Taj Mahal, in Agra, India, is one of the most famous buildings in the world.

The huge Alhambra palace, in Granada,
Spain, was built from 1238 to 1358.

In Spain, Muslims from North Africa known as
Andalusians, or Moors, founded great new cities
such as Cordoba and Granada. In Granada, they
built a spectacular fortified palace, called the
Alhambra, with lush gardens, ornate fountains,
and even flushing toilets.

Muslim traders introduced Islam to China, too,
where architects decorated buildings with
exquisite golden calligraphy.

This painting shows a group
of dervishes dancing in
traditional 'whirling skirts'.

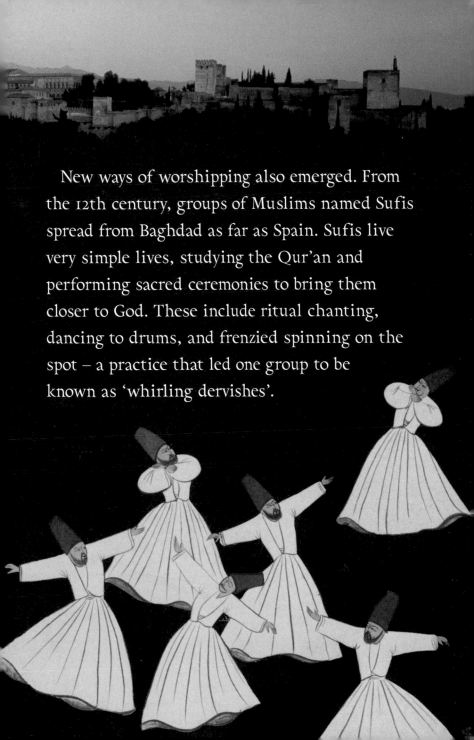

New ways of worshipping also emerged. From the 12th century, groups of Muslims named Sufis spread from Baghdad as far as Spain. Sufis live very simple lives, studying the Qur'an and performing sacred ceremonies to bring them closer to God. These include ritual chanting, dancing to drums, and frenzied spinning on the spot – a practice that led one group to be known as 'whirling dervishes'.

But during the 15th century, the story of Islam really focused on one city: Constantinople. Ever since the 5th century, it had been the great capital of the Christian Byzantine empire. Sitting between Europe and Asia, it was the most important trading city in the world – and one of the richest. Ships jostled for space in its bustling port, bringing goods from all over the globe.

By the middle of the century, though, the Byzantine rulers had lost most of their power. In 1453, a Turkish tribe of Sunni Muslims known as the Ottomans led a fierce attack on Constantinople.

The Ottoman sultan, Mehmet II, surrounded the city with 150,000 soldiers and 125 ships, blocking all escape. His army bombarded the walls with cannons so big it took 200 men to fire each one. The Byzantines held out for six weeks, but they were overwhelmed. Constantinople was taken by the Ottomans, and Mehmet renamed it Istanbul, which means 'to the city'. It became the glorious new heart of the Muslim world.

The walls of Constantinople were much larger than those shown
in this scene of the Ottoman army attacking the city in 1453.

Chapter 7

The magnificent Ottomans

Istanbul under the Ottomans grew into a spectacular city of art and culture, where artists from all over the world now came to live. The city's grandest Christian cathedral, the Hagia Sofia, was converted into a mosque, with towering minarets and lavish mosaics. Hundreds of new public baths were built, too, as well as schools for Muslim boys – named *medrasses* – and the Grand Bazaar, a market with over 4,000 stalls.

Mehmet II also built himself a lavish home, the Topkapi Palace, overlooking the port of Istanbul. Here, a group of over 300 beautiful female slaves, known as a harem, entertained the sultan with singing and exotic dancing whenever he chose.

This grand mosque in Istanbul, named the Hagia Sofia, was a cathedral before the Ottomans captured the city.

54

Like the Rightly Guided Caliphs of the 7th century, Mehmet and the next sultan, Selim, spread the word of the Qur'an by conquering new lands. Selim doubled the size of the Ottoman empire in ten years, invading most of Greece, as well as land in Persia belonging to a rival Shi'ite Muslim dynasty, the Safavids.

The crescent moon and star was originally an Ottoman symbol, but has since been used to represent all of Islam.

But the figure that most dominates Ottoman history is Selim's son, Suleiman, who became sultan in 1520. Suleiman regarded the growth of Christian powers in Europe as the greatest threat to Islam, so he set out to attack them.

His 200,000-strong army invaded most of Hungary, and the islands of Rhodes and Malta. In 1529, he reached as far as the city of Vienna, in Austria. Had he captured it, his army could have invaded all of Europe. But terrible winter weather forced him to turn back.

Suleiman also conquered most of the coast of North Africa, known as the Barbary Coast, and his navy dominated the Red Sea. He even hired savage Barbary pirates to terrorize Christian ships in the Mediterranean.

Taxes from these new lands made Suleiman the richest ruler in the world. Even the kings in Europe called him Suleiman the Magnificent.

By defeating Islam's enemies, Suleiman hoped to be seen as caliph of all Muslims. Because the Qur'an taught respect for other religions, Suleiman never forced Christians in his empire to convert to Islam. But he did demand that a fifth of all Christian males join his army. Many of these were trained from a young age to become elite fighters, known as janissaries. Riding into battle with white feathers in their hair, they were the most feared soldiers of their time.

Turkish horseman were trained to fire arrows at their enemies while still riding at full speed.

Suleiman used the Qur'an to guide him as ruler over his vast territories. Anybody was allowed to approach his imperial court, or divan, if they felt they were being treated unfairly. Criminals were also dealt with according to the law of the Qur'an. Thieves had their hands chopped off in public, or might be stoned to death. New punishments were invented too, such as impaling murderers on spikes. These were incredibly severe, but most people considered them to be fair. They named their sultan 'Suleiman the Lawgiver'.

This painting, of a criminal impaled on a hook, shows how severe punishments could be in the Ottoman empire.

But the richer Suleiman grew, the less interested he was in being seen as an ideal Muslim leader. He spent more and more time in his harem, where he became obsessed with an ambitious Russian slave named Roxelana.

Roxelana was the mother of four of Suleiman's sons, and was determined that the eldest would become the next sultan. She convinced the love-struck Suleiman that the son he'd had with another woman was plotting against him. The sultan had him strangled. When Suleiman died in 1566, Roxelana's son Selim gained control of the entire empire.

Suleiman is shown here practising archery in his palace.

But Selim was nothing like his father. He was fat and cowardly, and more interested in wine than the welfare of his people. He drank so much, he became known as Selim the Drunkard. In 1571, he even sent his navy to capture the island of Cyprus, simply because it was famous for its wine. But the fleet was completely destroyed by European ships near a place named Lepanto. It was the first big defeat for the Ottomans, and the start of a long period of decline.

The Ottoman empire lasted another 350 years, but later sultans were corrupt and incompetent. Some were even insane. Istanbul became less important as a base for trade, and the Ottoman empire grew weaker and weaker. By the 20th century, it was known as the Sick Man of Europe.

The final blow came after the First World War. The Ottomans sided with Germany, and after their defeat, most of their remaining lands were divided among the victorious nations. The last Ottoman sultan was overthrown in 1922, and Istanbul became part of the new republic of Turkey.

Chapter 8

Islam today

The decline of the Ottoman empire didn't slow down the growth of Islam. Today, there are around 1,400 million Muslims, roughly a quarter of the world's population. It's the second largest religion in the world, after Christianity, and also the fastest growing. As well as in the Middle East, there are huge Islamic communities in Indonesia, Bangladesh, Pakistan and India.

This minaret towers above a mosque in the modern city of Abu Dhabi, United Arab Emirates.

All Muslims are supposed to live their lives according to rules of conduct known as *shari'ah*, or the sacred law. The most important part of this is the Five Pillars of Islam, but the laws also deal with everyday matters such as marriage or banking.

Many Muslims interpret the *shari'ah* in different ways, such as how they dress, or the food that they eat. There also still remains a division between Shi'ite and Sunni Muslims, which began in the 7th century.

But, despite these differences, all Muslims consider themselves part of the same worldwide family, which they call the *ummah*, sharing a deep respect for their religion's glorious past.

Timeline of Islamic history

c. 610 - The prophet Muhammad receives his first revelation from God.

622 - Muhammad and the Muslims move to Medina. This is known as the Hijrah, and marks the first year of the Islamic calendar.

624 - The Muslims defeat the Meccans at the Battle of Badr.

630 - The Muslim army captures the city of Mecca for Islam.

632 - Muhammad dies in Medina, and an incredible period of Muslim military conquests begins under the four Rightly Guided Caliphs.

661 - The Umayyads declare themselves caliphs. During the next 200 years, the Islamic empire spreads as far as western Spain.

750 - The Abbasids defeat the Umayyads at the Battle of the Great Zab, and make Baghdad their new capital. The Golden Age of Islam begins.

1055 - The Seljuk Turks capture Baghdad, defeating the Abbasids.

1258 - Fierce Mongol warriors attack and destroy Baghdad. Later, Mongol leader Tamerlane creates a new Islamic capital at Samarkand. In India, his descendants form the Mughal empire.

1453 - The Turkish Ottoman ruler, Mehmet II, captures Constantinople and renames it Istanbul. His grandson, Suleiman I, becomes sultan in 1520 and rules over a great new Ottoman empire.

1571 - The Ottoman navy is defeated by Europeans at the naval Battle of Lepanto. The Ottoman empire starts to weaken.

1918 - The Ottoman empire is dissolved at the end of the First World War. Today, there are over 1,400 million Muslims, and Islam is the second largest religion in the world.

Index